Olivier Cadiot's

RED, GREEN AND BLACK

adapted from the French
by Charles Bernstein
& Olivier Cadiot

Potes & Poets Press Inc. Elmwood, Connecticut 1990

Sections of this work originally appeared in *Avec*, *The Washington Review of the Arts*, and *Serie d'Ecriture*.

Rouge, Vert & Noir by Olivier Cadiot was published by BLOCK Editions, Paris, in 1989, in conjunction with an exhibition of paintings by Bruno Carbonnet. *Rouge, Vert & Noir* was written in collaboration with these works; reproductions are included in the book. For more information, write BLOCK, 16, Impasse Gaudelet, 75001, Paris.

Cover by Susan Bee.

ISBN 0-937013-34-X

the roses
are they
red
in their obscurity?
one can decide to see
the roses red
in the obscurity

s is then how,

very struck by this arrow
so struck by this arrow

strike

very struck
so struck

strike

e said, for example

make, let, look, etc.

? (this cataclysm) I have read the description
? the cataclysm that I have read the description of

I read the description

"target"

?? the arrow has

touched the target

strike or touch

so much depends upon

constant
constant

a sole arrow

(*pierces*)

just one, each / just one each

the eyes closed
"ready to go" = on the point of parting
and see how

One recalls

the years past; all the days; the summer; the winter; Thurs
the final day; tomorrow; a day

forest
sky blue

one prepares and parts

the menace of rain

disperse/dispersed, open/opened

reunite, disperse, etc.

the rain
the rain

reunite, disperse, dissipate

e sky, the skies

(this idea) has flown

very clear

we part in three days

I ignore if this project pleases you

respond *toute suite*

y-es, y-es, y-es,

bytheveningsblūuvsummur

what then!

ta ta ta !

(silence.) dead silence. (grand silence.)

I will come; — I 've come

This is not all

is it that I part tomorrow,
will you come with me

the beautiful sky

grey, native

and essay a look

voluntarily

that reveals itself
*** that is itself revealed**

to me

appear, reveals, etc. ,

"void"
"void"

external, extreme, unique, etc.

of the same blow

a sole arrow,

when all's sunk

see, intend, sense

losing one's head

"void"
"void"

the role of profound objects, etc.

All's explained
All's explained

agreeable and evident

it is clear,

all's sunk

don't have fear, someone will get you out of it (= I will get yo
out of it, or maybe even: we will get you out of it)

to me

oh!

God!

"target"
"target"

the wind socks the trees. what is it that knocks the trees?

by the evenings blue of summer

the same causes produce the same effects

Enough noise; more for

in the sky blue

this is beautiful to see (= to be seen)

— "in the airs" —

the sky is
so blue, so

retain well this

the how, the when, the where, the why
enough, also, as much, a lot

better 'n' better

regret

***adieu*! pardon!**

AH!
Ha!
Oh!

appear, risk, etc.

I am certain to succeed

2 .

four fingers

the fingers expedited
1r, 3r and 4r
the thumb, the middle and pinkie
right) and 71 and 91
left) . With aid of a scalp

examine the rest

It was necessary to detach
the skin,

the end of each digit

injected
their contour at the extremities
each digit of which and took the fingerprints

and these red clothes
on these red clothes

hypothesis:

examines the dress
in the wat
sun faded the red
dead, thought that it was to be brig

ery seriously decomposed

disappeared and the animals
wrenched into little pieces
and that around the eyes and the ears
of the water herself
flesh
arms and the legs
remained intact

ome red dresses like this one?
ome red dresses, some dresses green, some dresses
ome dresses of all the colors

simply "of color"
the action of the water
worn out the clothes in spots
the rubbing against a stub or a
rock has provoked a tear

a somber stain
under

the dress

tissue
of nylon
cotton. Without sleeves, tailored
one must slip it
over the arms
and tie it up
there was besides
destined to receive
but nobody found a belt

—One can tell a stain
but that changes nothing
stains like that
stains like that
in order to say
stains like that

a dress like that
like a robe
like a dress

a side on the other
with a belt
loop of red thread

in the water

ertheless—
the time in the water

rule

post mortem
equivalent to two weeks
the soil

immersion

cause of death
the corpse float-
n the fresh water

a robe like that?

very (a robe very blue)?
so (a robe so blue)?
(the most blue robe)

3 .

introduction —>
a tiny pain (a minuscule doldrum)

That I die, that you die, that he dies

the rider *superbe*, the archer *magnifique*

1 . to see clear; — 2. to see clear indeed, more clear, less clear; — 3. to see very clear (most clear, really clear, etc .) — the most clear, the least clear

—I 'm absolutely set on it ! —well not me

—Yes. —Well! N

me!

—Oh not at all

no doubt, without doubt this won't be
Oh! Oh! I didn't take guard

rom here to tomorrow (time)

I have almost hit the deadline

your case will not be finished so fast

ey have said that (. . .)

a passed moment

ad; —2. also bad, the worst or more bad, less bad;—
very bad (really bad, so bad, etc.) —the worst, the most bad

did he cry? I cried louder (= if he cried, I cried louder)
should you refuse, I'll overrule (= in the case that you refuse, I overrule)

! : Hey! Hey! (or EH! EH!) you take it very haughtily!

if he had reflected,
if he had reflected, he'd've hesitated. if he's reflective.

we all sat; one of us stood

eh! : Hey! Eh! (or EH! EH!) you're getting real haughty!
it's you who wanted it (more strong, more insistent than: you wanted it)
did he cry out?
I cried louder (= if he cried out, I cried more)

Renounce (imperative) , I will not renounce (= if you renounc —me, I will not renounce)

1. much; —2. more (greater); —3. the
1. well; —2. so well, better, less well; —3. very well (well in —th

TRip, TRespass, TRemble

maritime, mortal, circular,

a) to cry out, to

[he cries with abandon]

a) torture; —b) pain very alive
(= live pain
extreme pain
dolor very bad)

weep

the chaser kills the chased

s, assuredly, without doubt,
YES truly, truly YES
yes, yes indeed

Yes

hat!

but no, etc.
h an air, with a tone,
iciant and taciturn, she responded distractedly
will go
a wink

the tempest vanishes, and the winds are calm

present?
m far: "Good day!" —How goes it? —Yes! —No!
these conditions

the end has come (. . .) ; *voilà*
in consequence of what, in consequence
ONLY (= nothing other than) cries

in the situation (. . .)

I saw, I sawed,
etc. that the vessel was sunk for two days.
I saw, I sawed, etc. , that the vessel will be sunk
within an hour
I saw, I sawed,
etc. , that the vessel sinks quick

no importance, little import
no import

no less than, no more than, no more

my face, as well as my soul

her face, as well as her heart

if he'd reflected, he'd've hesitated. if he's reflective, he hesit
if he'd reflected, he hesitates. if he's reflective, he'd've hesit

is black

in a manner confused
and disordered

Sweetly

this is so, this is good so
fast, quick, scarcely, in an instant
for the thing concerned

ah! my God!

sweetly; —2. oh so sweetly, more sweetly,
s sweetly; —3. very sweetly (indeed sweetly, so
eetly, etc.) —the most sweetly, the least sweetly

(such sweetness)

quite otherwise than for her
from others precisely as from you
t which (. . .) evades indefinitely to all others than you
from him to others
her eyes (. . .)

never ever, etc.

in my heart. —"I guard my heart"

by seeing: in order to have seen

ah well !

the remains of, that which remains of, that which there is of, that which I have of .

for example

1. little —2. oh so little, less; —3. very little (indeed little, so little, etc.)

(such littleness)

(. . .)

Nevertheless

God!

mystery

he fall of the day

confusion
I have regret to see you in error

I have regret

clusion
the hopefulness in many overcomes the dread

it follows

follows

"psst! "

makes us sad—> That saddens

first development

catastrophe/catastrophic—>

That could kill

4 .

metallic stitches introduced one by one

remove the sinews
and then section the tendon near where it is attache
—Open, on the metallic stitches,
all along the side. Then isolate

eye socket by the whole

lightly undulates in S
to 3 millimeters inside
at its cranial exit

The nerve

ahead and outdoors

In its trajectory
the optical nerve has its direction
penetrates in the eyeball
posterior pole. —It recoils

the vertical part
which the summit, or *angustia*, is to 1 millim
next makes a dilation
from where the horizontal portion begins. The conduits
by a common conduit
by two distinct orifices is exceptional

obliquely
Its superior convex face
reposes on the surface
—its anterior border
—its posterior border

egular

coloration very variable
of the blackening, presents a number of folds

spot circular and whitish of 1.5 millimeters
or *macula lutea*, of elliptical form,
at 3 millimeters outside

The spot, yellow,
situated at the posterior pole
ollow at its center of depression

free border

the whole surface
is divided by an indented (= serrated) line, circular,
the equator of the eye, and called *ora serrata*

tears are conducted

ard the free border of the eyelids
h of them is then divided
follows from inside to outside the free border
other turns away at the border's periphery
the former near the external angle of the eye

—Open

s not to break

often states similar to sleeping

Section the plan vertically
lift up the internal flap
remove
its deep surface and one also exposed

the eyes

free border

to enable to dissect more
In dissecting from top to bottom
it exists, a zone

If one wishes
somebody will preserve the two
of the eyelids, otherwise someone will remove them
easily the underlying plan

Incise

free border of eyelids; close up
in and on the outside. One
—Dissect the vessels
these are, from outside to inside

In order to
One must decide to make the cut

Before commencing

Extend
curved pin
which surrounds them, the muscles
internal border of the latter

reunite, disperse, dissipat

To make tilted
the fragment
One will see then all the face

ne will find it easily in this part or its trajectory

following a circular line

the incision
it is useful to uncover before
on a small part of its extent
up to this point or part
close-up in front and in back the two flaps. —Section

bove and inside
e origin

nervous toward its termination
(nerve ending)

to decide to make the cut,
one will examine the corpse

mortal, circular, etc.

ose-up the two flaps
ith precaution

so as not to break

then look for
and follow them

to some distance on the inside

5 .

at the site
corpse has been deposited, one (somebody) ren
the corpse
the world today, in default
has been retrieved
retrieved
and abandoned: worse!

astonishingly vague
of a chemise
dress
coverlet blue
"name: unknown"
unknown. Height:
hair: eyes:
age:
first name, that she's called

search
field of stalks
nothing
sky and earth
maritime, mortal, circular, etc.
nothing

to identify
since

motive. "after which all is possible." even
the secret "nothing's lost"
which goes bad
the dead
information which will come by us

mble and remember
more nothing to see
the more clear, the less clear
is who? In order to know who
"nothing's lost"

nothing more to see
necessity
is who? in order to know who

appeared
wrenched
wrenched
and that around the eyes

of the water herself
of flesh
arms & legs
somber

sombre
under
worn
the rubbing against
has provoked a tear
a stain
faded the red
in the water
that it was to be brighter

of her look
closed, then
charged with inventing how the child's e

would look
open, have been
circulated

diffused (circulate
primary care

at first to look for
child,
enfant,

dead, their reflex

retouched
firstly the eyes

primary care
firstly to look for
and one also exposed

risk to let this corpse

If somebody had wished to hide
someone had buried it

before conferring
(imperative)

six types of different hair

trace of earring
in the pockets of the dress

origin
grains of quartz
retrieved

same color of hair,
of eyebrows. detail
wrenched by the shooting

the age
by her ossification
evaluated.

blue drape,
the face

and eight small holes
contusions,

her look
"accidental"
equally disap-
pears) has made appear multiple
fracture, and for certain
rejoins

"target"
"target"

and will be long
today
and everyday nothing
reunite, disperse, etc.

6.

One has told me (one = someone: someone has told me
= somebody
has told me)

This is a happiness that you are here
(*good to see ya*)

just as he stopped talking, he sits

to make to fall
to push, that is throw down, demolish, that is
overturn, that is turn over
to ruin, that is to make to fall into pieces
to lower, decline, diminish

blind

nothing to dread when (. . .)
if (. . .) —We have not had

black

climate in: meandering
in: the woods where they were born

well the
—The water (. . .)
the water (. . .) source or (. . .) river

more black

we're here
the (noise, sound)

(repose, peace)
Ah! *trés beau*!
already, tomorrow, since, hencefor

(*Incroyable!*)
the grand invention, the finding
Ah *voilà*! An idea

(unheard of)
less black

than yours; —also, when one wants
as black as yours

very black

the river
to persevere, to escape, to expire, to stay
when
destiny that you've been menaced by
point indiscreetly
and you
n't
which dissipates itself

in the sky
baby blue
deep yellow, light yellow, dark green,

violet black, blood red

fly, run, go: avenge us
run, fly, be gone: we're avenged

it is to that (that which) I consent
this that (that which)
this is of that (that which) I'll speak later

One recalls
one prepares and parts

: memorize well that. Memorize th

some high poplars ornament the borders of the river

it snows, —it rains, —it thunder

among the trees, the most beautiful is the cedar
again: *voilà*! a little river

Horror! Ah!

and plunges deep into the water where (. . .)
touching it with the hand (. . .)

validates, vacates, vanishes,

—this word (. . .) escaped from me:
details (. . .) escaped me until now
sufferances
nothing more to see
necessity
is who?
in order to know who

extremity

(. . .) is soft and malleable
(. . .) but less
nctly. With the hand, and on top of that with the extremity of th
ers
(. . .) very sharp of things (. . .)

this is . . . that . . . , this is

then, today, beforehand, at once

this arrow
this flesh

hade, a shadow, a nothing

constant
constant

can, hope to, want to, would like to, desire to, demand to,
n to, decide to) leave now
think, believe, dread, tremble that, nearly found, have the
pression, am afraid, can't help that) I'm fainting

Psst!

Eh**bonjour**kids**

Les Kids
ze ze—little ones, ze
approach, halt!

"target"

This is [f]FORmidable! Ah! ze
[m]MISerable! ze [r]RIFFraff! Ug! ze [b]BANdits! --Everyday
dumb . . . He pronounces it ddumb

to see clear

clear (clear indeed, so clear etc)
disperse/disperses, open/opens

oh so clear, more clear, less clear

iny pain (. . .)
(a minuscule dolor)

cataclysm
cataclysm

it follows

conclusion

y seeing: in order to have seen

I love to look at green
bluish, greyish, reddish, greenish, whitish
(*noir*ish)

sometime, often, soon, everyday, late, early, etc.

of water
the taste of water
I see trees
the shadow of trees

the end is come (. . .) : *voilà*
catastrophe/catastrophic
in consequence of what, in consequence

the beautiful sky
grey, native

external, extreme, unique, etc.

the most little
the least
the most bad
the worst

time flows | **the river** | **the day** |

| **the river** | **the day** | **flows**

(silence.) dead silence. (grand silence.)

Ah! (joy, sadness) : ah! what good news!
Ha! (surprise) : ha! what you say!
Ug! (disgust): ug! the world!
Eh! (to call) : eh! over there!
Oy! (chagrin) : oy veh!
Oh! (to call) : oh! over there!

Potes & Poets Press, Inc.
181 Edgemont Avenue
Elmwood CT 06110

POTES AND POETS PRESS PUBLICATIONS

Miekal And, ***Book 7, Samsara Congeries***
Bruce Andrews, ***Excommunicate***
Bruce Andrews, ***from Shut Up***
Todd Baron, ***Dark as a hat***
Dennis Barone, ***Forms / Froms***
Dennis Barone, ***The World / The Possibility***
Lee Bartlett, ***Red Scare***
Beau Beausoleil, ***in case / this way two things fell***
Steve Benson, ***Reverse Order***
Steve Benson, ***Two Works Based on Performance***
Brita Bergland, ***form is bidden***
Charles Bernstein, ***Amblyopia***
Charles Bernstein, ***Conversation with Henry Hills***
Julia Blumenreich, ***Parallelism***
John Byrum, ***Cells***
Abigail Child, ***A Motive for Mayhem***
Norman Cole, ***Metamorphopsia***
Clark Coolidge, ***A Geology***
Clark Coolidge, ***The Symphony***
Cid Corman, ***Essay on Poetry***
Cid Corman, ***Root Song***
Beverly Dahlen, ***A Reading (11-17)***
Tina Darragh, ***a(gain)2st the odds***
Tina Darragh, ***Exposed Faces***
Alan Davies, ***a an av es***
Alan Davies, ***Mnemonotechnics***
Alan Davies, ***Riot Now***
Jean Day, ***from No Springs Trail***
Ray DiPalma, ***The Jukebox of Memnon***
Ray DiPalma, ***New Poems***
Rachel Blau DuPlessis, ***Drafts #8 and #9***
Rachel Blau DuPlessis, ***Tabula Rosa***
Johanna Drucker, ***from Bookscape***
Theodore Enslin, ***Case Book***
Theodore Enslin, ***Mediations on Varied Grounds***
Theodore Enslin, ***September's Bonfire***
Norman Fischer, ***The Devices***

Steven Forth, *Calls This*
Peter Ganick, *Met Honest Stanzas*
Peter Ganick, *Rectangular Morning Poem*
Peter Ganick, *Two Space Six*
Robert Grenier, *What I Believe*
Carla Harryman, *Vice*
Carla Harryman, *The Words*
Susan Howe, *Federalist 10*
Janet Hunter, *in the absence of alphabets*
P. Inman, *backbite*
P. Inman, *Think of One*
P. Inman, *waver*
Andrew Levy, *Reading Places, Reading Times*
Jackson Mac Low, *Prose & Verse from the Early 80's*
Jackson Mac Low, *Twenties (8-25)*
Barbara Moraff, *Learning to Move*
Laura Moriarty, *the goddess*
Janette Orr, *The Balcony of Escape*
Jena Osman, *Ellerby's Observatory*
Gil Ott, *Public Domain*
Maureen Owen, *Imaginary Income*
Keith Rahmings, *Printouts*
Dan Raphael, *The Matter What Is*
Dan Raphael, *Oops Gotta Go*
Dan Raphael, *Zone du Jour*
Stephen Ratcliffe, *Sonnets*
Joan Retallack, *Western Civ Cont'd*
Maria Richard, *Secondary Image / Whisper Omega*
Susan Roberts, *cherries in the afternoon*
Susan Roberts, *dab / a calling in*
Kit Robinson, *Up Early*
Leslie Scalapino, *clarinet part I heard*
Leslie Scalapino, How Phenomena Appear to Unfold
Laurie Schneider, *Pieces of Two*
Spencer Selby, *Accident Potential*
Gail Sher, *w/*
James Sherry, *Lazy Sonnets*
Ron Silliman, *B A R T*
Ron Silliman, *Lit*
Ron Silliman, *from Paradise*
Pete Spence, *Almanak*
Pete Spence, *Elaborate at the Outline*
Diane Ward, *Being Another / Locating in the World*
Diane Ward, *Crossing*
Craig Watson, *The Asks*
Hannah Weiner, *Nijole's House*